Let's Declare Ourselves Winners
...and Get the Hell Out

Books by Bill Mauldin

Let's Declare Ourselves Winners...and Get the Hell Out
Mud and Guts
The Brass Ring
Up Front
I've Decided I Want My Seat Back
What's Got Your Back Up?
Bill Mauldin in Korea
Bill Mauldin's Army (reprinted 1983)
A Sort of a Saga
Back Home
Star Spangled Banter
Up Front
This Damn Tree Leaks
Mud, Mules and Mountains

Let's Declare Ourselves Winners...
and Get the Hell Out

★
PRESIDIO

Published by Presidio Press, 31 Pamaron Way, Novato, CA 94947

Library of Congress Cataloging in Publication Data

Mauldin, Bill, 1921
    Let's declare ourselves winners—and get the hell out.

    1. United States—Politics and government—1977-1981—
Caricatures and cartoons.   2. United States—Politics and
government—1981-   —Caricatures and cartoons.   3. American
wit and humor, Pictorial.
I. Title.
E872.M28   1985   973.926   85-9475
ISBN 0-89141-115-1

To Chris

Preface

Recently I ran into a colleague who said, "I see you went back to your old style a couple or three years ago." He was referring to the crayon *cum* brush technique sharp-eyed readers will note in the latter part of this book, compared to the simple black-and-white brush work in the beginning.

In my opinion many cartoonists, especially younger ones, concern themselves over-much with "style" and ornate signatures when their time would be better spent improving their ideas. If an artist cooks up a good idea and executes it properly, his "style" will take care of itself.

Actually, my various "styles," such as they are, have been strictly the products of necessity. For example, in wartime Sicily and Italy forty-odd years ago, engravers' equipment was worn out or wrecked, making it impossible for them to reproduce fine lines or fancy shading. So I drew heavy, bold, contrasty lines that even a cracked lens couldn't miss. The fact that this resulted in an appropriate and distinctive "style" for wartime drawings was not due to any inspiration on my part—it was simple expediency.

For thirty years or so after the war I went back to using crayons for tonality, because stark black-and-white seemed too harsh and uncompromising for civilian subjects, especially politics, which, after all, we are told is the very art of compromise.

And then, during the late 70s, I was away from the office most of the time, often thousands of miles away, and found the mail too slow. Taking advantage of technology, I began transmitting drawings over the telephone, first by Telecopier and then by Laser-photo. At best such contraptions have approximately the reproductive capability of a Sicilian copy camera dug from the rubble. And so I was forced back to my heavy, simple "style" of yore. (Actually, I enjoy the looseness and freedom of drawing that way, but it is still too contrasty for politics.) Then in the early 80s I discovered Federal Express and was able to go back to my crayon and still make my deadlines.

So much for "style." As for the contents of this book, the cartoons cover the last of the Jimmy Carter years and most of the Ronald Reagan years so far. They honestly reflect my opinions, at least as of the publication dates shown with the drawings. (Hell, man, these are changing times.)

I always try to be both clever and concise, often succeeding at neither, but have generously tried to weed out most of the turkeys. I apologize for those that sneaked past.

Bill Mauldin

"These long orbits give me a chance to fix my shoes."

January 1, 1978

February 3, 1978

Things were tough all over in 1978. A dollar was hard to come by and wouldn't buy much when you found it.

February 23, 1978

My first disillusionment with Jimmy Carter, who carried his own bag and had walked humbly to his inauguration, was when he failed to cut down the size of the White House fleet of luxurious jetliners. I'm still waiting for Reagan to do it.

"...If we could only find a way to dramatize the fuel crisis..."

2

March 2, 1978

After the famous *Playboy* interview about lust in his heart Jimmy kept a low profile, sinwise, leaving it to his number two man to throw sticky drinks into the faces of barroom critics.

"Ham Jordan is my surrogate sinner."

March 8, 1978

"Who stole my snowman's shiny black eyes?"

3

"*This year the pigeons are feeding her.*"

March 30, 1978

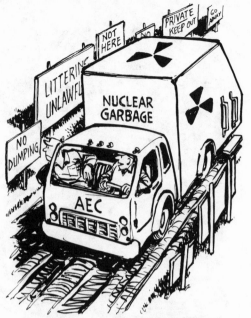

May 3, 1978

The same day I drew this cartoon I wrote a little piece suggesting obsolete old ICBMs be loaded with radioactive waste and sent into the sun. NASA sent me a declassified study of the concept, saying it would work but would cost electrical consumers about five percent more. End of idea.

"Maybe we could package it as a soil conditioner."

May 10, 1978

The revolutionaries of my youth were upwardly mobile poor kids who became young Republicans after they'd acquired a few bucks. How do you deal with crazies who start rich?

"I'm bored with kidnaping. Let's drag-race our Ferraris."

May 26, 1978

The kind of egotist who becomes a head of any government likes to assume that when *he* dies it will be *Götterdämmerung*. Hooray for the neutron bomb. It might give the trigger-men a sense of relative values.

"They could kill us without wrecking the Kremlin? Horrible!"

June 5, 1978

"Why make trouble? Don't you like détente?"

6

*"No doubt about it.
Living causes cancer."*

June 14, 1978

June 22, 1978

To me the great charm of the Israelis when I was there before, during, and after the Six Day War was that they disliked militarism but knew how to handle it. I wondered if eventually all those wars might turn them into Spartans. To a degree it seems to have happened.

Endangered Species

7

July 26, 1978

Firestone had a great alibi for building those radial tires that blew above 55 mph. They could have said they were merely supporting the law. They didn't say it.

"So what's the beef? You got two tires for the price of one."

August 7, 1978

Nobody ever had better *intentions* than Jimmy Carter. He really *wanted* more women in important jobs. The times just weren't ripe.

"Just change it back to 'mop closet.'"

August 30, 1978

We Americans love to help kick out rascals such as the Shah of Iran or the dictator of Nicaragua. Then we turn our backs until new rascals surface.

Every rule has an end.

September 8, 1978

A further example of Jimmy's good-heartedness was his apparent determination to sink the navy before some foreign power could beat him to it.

"Tora! Tora! Tora!"

September 14, 1978

In a society where car is king, what to do when car turns killer? Ford Pintos were cremating their occupants after comparatively minor rear-end collisions. Whom to blame? Finally the Ford Motor Company itself was indicted for homicide.

"You have the right to remain silent…"

November 22, 1978

Jim Jones, a bush-league messiah, wasn't satisfied to be a prophet for profit. He had to go and take himself seriously, taking some 900 followers in Guyana along with him via the suicide route.

"Religious zealots are giving us all a bad name."

"We had better do as it says."

December 20, 1978

After almost three decades, China opened its doors to American enterprise and ad men. Talk about a captive audience!

"We did a little exploratory surgery, Doc."

December 28, 1978

January 11, 1979

Joe Califano, a veteran bureaucrat serving as Carter's Health, Education, and Welfare secretary, quit cigarets. As a cabinet-grade official he naturally expected the nation to quit with him.

"That Califano will stop at nothing."

February 6, 1979

"All that parading wore it out."

February 21, 1979

For the first time since our departure things were really beginning to heat up in Southeast Asia.

14

February 26, 1979

The Chinese, who of all people should have known better, decided to show the recently departed Americans how to *properly* invade Vietnam.

March 12, 1979

People tend to underestimate the Vietnamese because the little cusses are so cute.

"Anybody else in a spanking mood?"

15

*"They won't get far. That's an odd plate
and this is an even day."*

April 11, 1979

Remember how California worked out a clever method of fuel rationing?

16

May 17, 1979

In certain parts of the U.S. there was no real shortage of fuel, if you didn't mind burning the stuff instead of drinking it.

May 29, 1979

Skylab began falling out of orbit in pieces. After much computer-scanning NASA announced that probably nobody would get trashed but Australia.

...No damage to persons or property. (News Item)

June 5, 1979

Sadat tied himself down by going along with Jimmy Carter's "peace process." Then Menachem Begin turned the ants loose.

SETTLEMENTS

June 6, 1979

Carter put a new twist on the mountaineer's credo: "I must strip-mine it because it's there."

"Men drivers!"

June 19, 1979

Maggie Thatcher, a conservative, took charge of what was left of the British Empire. (As a fancier of fine machinery I found it genuinely painful to wreck a Rolls-Royce, even in a drawing.)

June 20, 1979

The Vietnamese, having blood-ied the noses of two superpowers in succession, decided to try a little imperialism themselves in Cambodia. Why not? They couldn't let all that captured U.S. military equipment rust.

"What will Jane Fonda think of you now?"

August 12, 1979

One of the first things Khomeini did in Iran was to put women back into what he considered to be their place.

"My wife was a nag, too, until the Ayatollah had her shot."

20

"I attacked him because he looked like a lame duck."

August 28, 1979

While the Ayatollah was proving himself a hard-nose, Jimmy Carter seemed determined to go the other way. Nobody will ever know if he was really attacked by a rabbit, but it seemed believable.

21

August 29, 1979

Almost every time the Soviets sent a batch of performing artists abroad, they pulled the cage back in and found a few birds missing.

"If you want to dance abroad you'll have to get used to it."

September 16, 1979

As U.S. blacks drew closer to Islam, and Israel, under the dour Menachem Begin, seemed bent upon blowing its hard-won reservoir of international good will, an old and productive alliance began coming apart in America.

"Mommy! Daddy!"

October 14, 1979

Begin became too much even for Moishe Dayan, a giant in Israel's history who had distinguished himself not only as a war hero but as a man who was not insensitive to the Arabs.

*"So who needs you?
The steering wheel is
locked anyway."*

October 17, 1979

We've all become used to advertising by "semi-doctors": chiropractors, optometrists, etc. But when real, bonafide MD's began appearing in TV and newspaper ads and hanging out neon shingles, a lot of people went into shock.

November 4, 1979

Overworked police have become drawn more and more into enforcing blue-nose laws instead of chasing real criminals. In New York City cops stopped responding to burglary reports and advised callers simply to tell it to their insurance companies.

"Sorry, we're tied up. Report prowlers to your local vigilante group."

November 14, 1979

"I couldn't afford a hospital or a funeral, so I got better."

24

"You show great clarity of vision, my son."

December 5, 1979

When the Ayatollah Khomeini violated one of the most sacred of international laws and sent his young hoodlums into the U.S. embassy in Teheran, Ted Kennedy passed up a golden opportunity to keep quiet. He said the Shah had been pretty bad himself, ignoring the fact that the Shah hadn't kidnapped an embassy full of Americans.

25

"Looks like we just bought a Chrysler."

January 1, 1980

In our economy bad management leads to bankruptcy—unless you're a big enough company.

January 14, 1980

The late Senator "Scoop" Jackson once said the Soviets conduct foreign policy like a hotel burglar, trying each door in the hallway until they find one unlocked. In Afghanistan they felt they had found an open door.

"Win their hearts and minds or blow off their heads."

January 16, 1980

In a rare display of outrage, Jimmy Carter slapped a grain embargo on Russia and pulled us out of the Moscow Summer Olympics, along with some of our stauncher allies.

Summer Olympics

27

February 4, 1980

You've got to hand it to the Arabs: unlike the South Koreans they use their own money to bribe us.

"You can buy any sort of favor in these banana republics."

March 19, 1980

President Carter seemed to have used his entire ration of intestinal fortitude upon the Russians. The Iranians got away with one outrage after another against their American hostages. When I drew this cartoon, of course, I didn't realize that Jimmy was cooking up a sort of rescue attempt, which sort of didn't work.

"If this turkey finds out he's an eagle, I'm in trouble."

28

March 20, 1980

Iranians weren't the only people looking for messiahs. Many Americans, starved for leadership, felt a hasty fluttering of the heart over John Anderson.

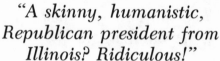

"A skinny, humanistic, Republican president from Illinois? Ridiculous!"

April 11, 1980

Deprived of the Russian grain market, many American farmers felt pushed to the brink. (This cartoon was a takeoff on one I had done forty years earlier about the horse cavalry becoming mechanized. I was tired of other cartoonists stealing it and decided to steal it back.)

29

May 5, 1980

Jimmy seemed to have no positive plans for saving the economy...

"They say you sink faster if you struggle."

May 16, 1980

...But he did have a missile. The problem was he didn't have a place to put it.

"Why not plant MX missiles here and save all that digging?"

"Nobody left but smart Russians and dumb Cubans, sir."

May 17, 1980

Castro suddenly made us a present of all the tens of thousands of citizens he couldn't stand any more: everybody from pickpockets to political dissidents.

"*How'd you like to be members of a persecuted majority?*"

May 26, 1980

May 27, 1980

One of several peculiarities about us Americans is the fact that we treat our wars like games (woe to the losing players) and our games like wars.

"Ya think this is some kinda game? Get out there an' WIN!"

June 12, 1980

Airline deregulation might have been a shot in the arm for free enterprise, but it was a pain in the neck for travellers.

"When all else fails, haggle."

June 13, 1980

*"Ugliest damn snow
I ever saw."*

June 16, 1980

Maggie Thatcher joined an international chorus urging Begin to deal with the Palestinians.

*"I fail to understand your
reluctance to sit down
with terrorists."*

June 18, 1980

Military morale reached a new low during the Carter administration. So did effective service income as inflation soared. Some German citizens even started making up "CARE" packages for needy families of American troops overseas.

"Don't under-tip your company commander, son."

June 24, 1980

The day was long gone when all you needed for national defense was a mob of low-I.Q., ill-paid cannon fodder.

"Our $2 per hour crew chief screwed up our $20 million bird."

35

July 3, 1980

Carter's cumulative fumbles began to suggest a political possibility which up to now had been, to Democrats at least, a laughable fantasy.

"I hear they might turn it into an old actor's home."

July 21, 1980

The last bright hope of the liberals floated brilliantly across the horizon and sank like a lead soap bubble in the sunset...

"You don't seem to have much to declare, after all."

"I made a lot of money today, dear."

August 28, 1980

. . . and inflation continued apace. The price of gold skyrocketed, candy bars approached a half-dollar each, and grandma's jewelry began coming out of the vault, piece by piece.

September 23, 1980

Iraq went to war with Iran and the Ayatollah blamed it all, of course, upon "satanic America." This took some pretty tangled thinking because of our ties to Israel, which Iraq hated even more than Iran...but logic and fanaticism never did mix.

"I recognize you under your clever disguise, Jimmy Carter."

September 26, 1980

Meanwhile, we made another of our own little contributions to stability on the other side of the world.

"Naturally, you'll use it for peaceful purposes..."

October 7, 1980

Sensing electoral victory, Ronald Reagan continued to commit himself to saving the country, but in the broadest general terms.

"At least mine sort of runs..."

November 4, 1980

One of Reagan's favorite promises was to liberate the enterprise he sensed lurking in the recesses of every citizen's soul.

"I can hardly wait for government to start getting off my back."

39

November 6, 1980

Well, anyway, the election was over and the Republicans sure did get the Carter bunch off our backs.

"Billy who?"

November 14, 1980

December 2, 1980

"They're gonna have to put us to work or send us to war."

December 12, 1980

Reports out of Russia made it increasingly clear that the newly compassionate state was using sanity hearings instead of firing squads. Labor camps could now be called funny farms, and making little rocks out of big ones would be occupational therapy.

"Nuts are for cracking."

41

December 13, 1980

U.S. industry and labor reacted with customary sportsmanship and fighting spirit to foreign competition...

"I demand a rematch with one of his hands tied."

December 14, 1980

...and we kept piling up indebtedness to some other foreigners who were simply robbing us blind.

The Light at the End of the Tunnel

"Don't waste food. Think of all the hungry Americans."

December 25, 1980

43

January 1, 1981

With his party back in power, Henry Kissinger surfaced on many talk shows, giving multitudinous answers to ponderous questions.

"Please tremble a little for old times' sake."

SALE
$99,000
CALL 555-4151

January 2, 1981

No matter what Reagan might actually do about inflation after his inauguration, for the moment it continued to run wild on its own.

"You haven't referred to house trailers as eyesores lately."

January 15, 1981

The Russians relieved some of our depressed economic mood by providing us with a bit of grim amusement as they bogged down, American-style, in their own "easy little war."

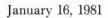

"Let's declare ourselves winners and get the hell out."

January 16, 1981

Reagan made the most momentous of several controversial cabinet choices. Poor Kissinger! Maybe he had shot his wad on all those talk shows.

"I hope he scares Russia as much as he scares me."

"We did it! We finally conquered the world!"

January 20, 1981

February 3, 1981

Was this it? Was this the opening shot in the crusade against the monster that was devouring us all?

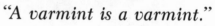

"A varmint is a varmint."

February 10, 1981

February 25, 1981

"*I want to see the roads
out of Washington choked
with refugees.*"

"*Couldn't you wait
till I set it?*"

March 2, 1981

Our new president lost no time in making clear his policy toward left-wing revolutions in our hemisphere. It began to look as if our sardonic grin at Russian armed intervention in Afghanistan might be quickly wiped off our faces.

"Damn right you do."

March 24, 1981

Facing an obviously unsympathetic administration, our modern-day suffragettes gamely fought on.

March 30, 1981

Reagan the horse-opera actor actually got shot, and conducted himself with aplomb which brought cheers from all sides.

April 1, 1981

Firearms abolitionists tried to exploit the attempted assassination, but Reagan pointed out that had existing laws been applied (his assailant had tried to board an airliner with two pistols and was not prosecuted) the guy would already have been out of circulation.

"The way to stop this madness is by outlawing rocks."

50

April 15, 1981

Of course, *some* people really ought to have their weapons confiscated, but they seem to be out of the abolitionists' jurisdiction.

"Go shoot some Afghans and you'll feel better."

April 21, 1981

"We call the small tactical model our Saturday Night Special."

April 29, 1981

May 15, 1981

"This takes all the fun out of working for the government."

May 26, 1981

"The answer is to draft everybody over sixty."

June 9, 1981

Israelis have always had a marvelous knack for solving certain kinds of strategic and tactical problems with lightning moves and minimal loss of life. The only casualty in the nocturnal removal of Iraq's French-built nuclear facility was a French technician who could reasonably have been expected to have gone home at quitting time.

"Don't cry, mon cher — *I'll sell you another."*

June 10, 1981

"The Israelis say they don't take contracts."

June 11, 1981

"I say...how does all the riffraff keep getting in?"

June 12, 1981

The Ayatollah Khomeini, in deep trouble from his war against Iraq, again demonstrated his talent for finding scapegoats. President Bani-Sadr, a faithful follower with a face out of a joke store, went the way of all Khomeini's close associates.

"That's the difference between being president and chairman of the board."

July 14, 1981

The Mediterranean fruit fly was eating California alive. Governor Brown, a dedicated environmentalist, didn't want to tamper with God's work. Also, he feared the antidote might eat holes in his constituents. In the end though, Jerry bowed to public pressure and sprayed all over without the loss of a single voter.

"Never mind the fruit flies—did you get Jerry Brown?"

July 29, 1981

Reagan, an old Brown antagonist, had his own way of dealing with troublesome pests.

"You're cleared to land."

July 30, 1981

Menachem Begin, an enthusiastic varmint-hunter himself, got a little careless with his illegal use of American equipment in Lebanon.

"Who ordered a navigator?"

July 31, 1981

The British royal family, always noted for showmanship, spliced Charles and Diana in a gala that diverted the world for days.

"Everybody needs a little pomp and pageantry."

August 7, 1981

Indulging in a little showmanship of its own, the Reagan administration made clear its feeling that the pendulum had swung too far in favor of clean air and water at the expense of industry.

Dirty Old Man

September 2, 1981

Even as the Reagan Revolution clanked on, its main target, inflation, continued to have a life of its own.

"Ten more years and our bank loot won't be worth digging up."

September 15, 1981

Grimly, the battle escalated. Apparently you can't brew coffee without breaking some crutches.

September 16, 1981

Even stockbrokers begged for mercy and looser money from the mint, but the New Right was giving no quarter.

"Those editors think we'll swallow anything."

As I was going up the stair
I met a man who wasn't there.
He wasn't there again today.
I wish, I wish he'd stay away.

(Hughes Mearns)

September 24, 1981

Another war, this one from a decade before, came back to haunt the government. If there was a moral to the Agent Orange saga, it was that those who spray should be made to pay.

October 7, 1981

Unfortunately, the point seems to have been lost on some chemical companies...and Bhopal hadn't even happened yet.

"The fruit is from Costa Roca, where your company sells pesticides."

October 10, 1981

Even narcs now admit privately to friends that the great anti-marijuana crusade is even more futile, wasteful, and self-defeating than was booze prohibition earlier in the century.

"If we had brains we'd stop fighting it and start taxing it."

October 16, 1981

Society does, however, sometimes try to protect itself from something it perceives as a genuine threat...

Critical Mass

61

October 19, 1981

...or someone it considers a genuine jerk.

"Beautiful view. Can we hide it from Secretary Watt?"

"Care for a last lollipop?"

October 20, 1981

Ayatollah executes dissidents down to nine years old.
(News Item)

"*Well, at least we seem to have united Europe.*"

October 21, 1981

November 9, 1981

Not only is David Stockman fun to draw, he's fun to watch. He likes to see how far he can go without getting stomped. In a magazine interview he confessed that Reaganomics was a big word for trickle-down. Obviously the boss needs him more than vice versa.

December 8, 1981

Qadhafi allegedly sent a hit team to knock off prominent American politicians, thereby spreading terror across our land. Since the two aims don't jibe, nothing came of the plot.

"Visitors from Libya, hey? Business or pleasure?"

December 15, 1981

The IRS embarked upon one of its own little terror campaigns to convince citizens of its omnipotence.

"Sorry, lady. He's a licensed mugger."

December 18, 1981

One of the IRS's favorite tactics is to seize and padlock small businesses, thereby demonstrating its capability for utter ruthlessness. I'm convinced.

"Shouldn't we leave his pencils so he can make more money?"

December 24, 1981

"I hate to think we're kin to a bunch of Bible-thumpers."

"How about a candle for us, Señor?"

December 25, 1981

It has been a revelation to watch every union-buster in the Western world rally around in support of Solidarity and the rights of working stiffs against tyranny. In another hemisphere, of course.

"Nuknak here has neat ideas about
putting pensioners on ice floes."

January 1, 1982

January 11, 1982

"I negotiate airline tickets through my bookie now."

New Industrial Revolution

January 13, 1982

This made a very pretty picture for a while. I wish both parties would frame it and refer to it from time to time.

January 20, 1982

*"Four dollars a pound?
Outrageous!"*

February 20, 1982

After watching the news and reading serious articles about how today's hard dollar distresses our allies and exporters, I still prefer it to our recent soft dollar.

*"Save those U.S. dollars,
boys—the Yankees might
rise again."*

69

March 5, 1982

As a non-jock who never reads sports pages, I worry sometimes that I should broaden my horizons. An obvious case of collusion between Valenzuela's bosses and U.S. Immigration gave me my chance: a civil rights issue plus an excuse to draw a sports cartoon. Inevitably, I put the ball in Lefty Valenzuela's right hand. Back to the old dugout.

"One strike and yer out."

March 8, 1982

Sometimes the Third World seems to forget that the First World didn't get there totally by accident, inheritance, or inability to adapt.

March 10, 1982

The United Auto Workers had made concessions to help their moribund industry. But now they detected faint new stirrings of life in Detroit and were already preparing to hit the streets with picket signs to get their hallowed privileges back. And now they faced a new problem: robots.

"I am trying to learn all phases before I take over."

March 24, 1982

The economy really was beginning to perk up under Reagan, but many businessmen had settled into a paralyzing habit of feeling sorry for themselves under the real and imagined poundings they had been taking.

"On your feet, man! I'm trying to set you free! Free!"

71

"Like to have your lawn fertilized by a Ph.D.?"

April 1, 1982

Signs of a reviving economy were obvious to brighter members of the younger set, but meanwhile a guy had to eat.

"Will it be integrated?"

April 6, 1982

One sometimes had the comforting feeling that much of Reaganism was a show for his ultra-right constituency, but there was no doubt about where he stood on busing.

Day of the Jackal

April 7, 1982

Poor old Britain seemed so far down the tubes that Argentina decided to lay claim to a few sub-Arctic hummocks flying the Union Jack some 400 gusty miles offshore.

74

April 8, 1982

Bully for the British. Rising painfully and goutily but manfully to the occasion, they made clear from the outset that the two-bit display of Argentine *macho* was foredoomed.

"The good news is that there's plenty of mutton."

April 20, 1982

"I'll miss you, too."

"But I didn't send for an exterminator."

June 6, 1982

On another side of the world from the Falklands another invasion was moving along. Begin wasn't about to let a few Lebanese get in the way of his hot pursuit of the P.L.O.

76

"Got him!"

June 14, 1982

June 18, 1982

The Russians made an unexpected announcement which seemed magnanimous until we counted some 25,000 of their tanks in East Germany alone.

Fine Print

June 16, 1982

"We can't remove Solidarity without removing Poland."

*"I have the final solution to
the Palestinian problem."*

June 22, 1982

As his armor and air force (using blockbusters and U.S.-built anti-personnel cluster bombs) clobbered the cornered Palestinians and everything near them in Beirut, Begin came to Washington to explain things to Reagan.

June 24, 1982

Japanese computer companies sent some sneaky fellows prowling into our computer companies. It was just like the old times when they renamed a city so they could stamp "Made in USA" on goods manufactured there.

"The Japanese have decided our secrets are worth stealing again."

June 30, 1982

"First we'll have to get rid of the old man."

July 6, 1982

A few years back the Capitol was rocked with scandals involving kinky congressmen and page boys. Now it was cocaine. Honest bourbon slurpers had to watch their language.

"All I said was let's have a snort in the cloakroom."

July 7, 1982

Poor Reagan wanted to be a new Teddy Roosevelt and wave a big stick. However, Teddy didn't have to contend with so many eager stick-eaters.

July 8, 1982

Latin American armies have never been noted for kindness to their troops, even when they've won. When Argentina's defeated soldiers trickled home from the Falklands, it looked for a while as if the home folks weren't even going to let them in.

Unknown Soldiers

July 19, 1982

The oath of Hippocrates does not include vows of poverty and no good American wants to see retreaded tires on his family doctor's Mercedes.

"Medicare takes good care of us medics."

July 22, 1982

Well, it's nice to know somebody is getting richer than the
sawbones.

"Go-o-od boy!"

July 28, 1982

"On the other hand..."

"I liked our old underdog image."

August 3, 1982

August 6, 1982

So far there have been no massive spills of radioactive material along our poorly maintained railroad rights-of-way, but maybe that's because they seldom carry any. They've spilled everything else.

"I spliced in a 2x4 until we can get a new rail."

September 24, 1982

Soviets include Cuban in cosmonaut team.
(News Item)

85

October 6, 1982

A Soviet submarine was spotted while snooping in Scandinavian waters. It gave everybody a merry chase until it was able to escape.

*"What are you looking for—
the Nobel Peace Prize?"*

*"That last fix was
dynamite. Got any more?"*

October 8, 1982

The prime rate was allowed to drop a fraction and the stock market went ape, like a spring compressed too long.

October 24, 1982

*"...But we make the
world's finest tanks."*

November 1, 1982

*"More grain, you
godless barbarian?"*

November 2, 1982

The problem of where to put all those MX's was getting desperate. The Pentagon wasn't listening to people offering the most imaginative suggestions.

"We've got to hide 'em someplace."

November 3, 1982

The stock market continued its optimism despite the fact that we were still in recession. *But were we?* Could Reaganomics be actually beginning to work? Stick around, folks.

November 11, 1982

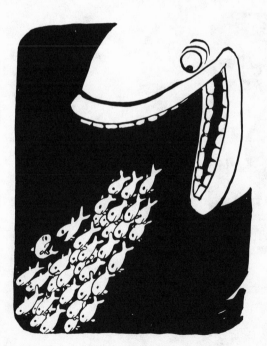

"We call it 'dense-pack.'"

November 23, 1982

Even if he turned out to be right about economics, this aspect of Reagan's planning left a lot to be desired. He was going to put all the MX's into a tight little bunch so all the missiles aimed at them would presumably collide with each other.

December 13, 1982

"Why do they call them-
selves 'public' utilities?"

December 16, 1982

"Well, at least we've taken a
little of the commercialism
out of Christmas."

December 20, 1982

It began to look as if the man who shot the Pope was part of an Eastern European conspiracy. Eastern European conspiracies were rotten enough before the KGB came along to take charge. Now nothing is safe or sacred.

"Careful...there's a Bulgarian contract out on you."

December 29, 1982

Since the Russian people are never told any bad news about Afghanistan, you wonder what the Red Army really does with all those bodies.

"...Another uncensored war bulletin from Afghanistan."

"Who? Me?"

January 7, 1983

To hear truckers tell it, they merely use their big rigs to roll those interstates smooth for passenger cars.

February 7, 1983

There was now no question about it. Reaganomics had begun to work for a lot of people. Maybe in time it would work for more of them.

"Sure it's moving, but did you see the length of that rope?"

*"It was a small holocaust, followed by
a small amount of justice."*

February 15, 1983

Lebanese Christians, who were clients of the Israelis, machine-gunned hundreds of unarmed Palestinian refugees, including women and children, in their camps. For a while the world was reminded of Nuremburg: Begin said he didn't know what was going on and Sharon was just following orders.

February 17, 1983

"I had a good EPA job until they found out I could actually see."

February 23, 1983

"You'll look great in arms control, you'll go to E.P.A., you to the U.N...."

94

Good Neighbor Policy

March 2, 1983

"I'll give you an environment you won't mind having blown up."

March 17, 1983

March 18, 1983

Inevitably, the government's quixotic war against the Great Satan Cannabis
had to degenerate into something called "Crimestoppers," an attempt to turn
our children into a society of informers.

April 7, 1983

Cartoonists are often asked why they can't say something nice about some-body. Okay, here's a man I truly admire. Against every pressure (including plenty from nervous Reaganites) he stood firm and brought inflation to a screeching halt.

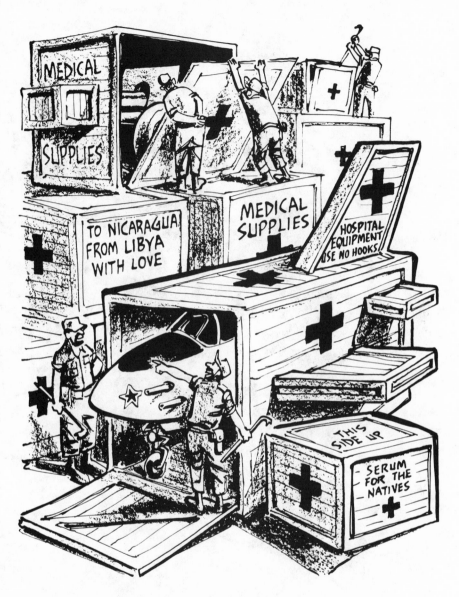

"The ammunition is in the crate marked 'Tranquilizers.'"

April 22, 1983

*"Of course we have our own peace movemen
Here he is."*

April 13, 1983

May 4, 1983

The American Catholic hierarchy, in agreement with our president on such matters as abortion and religion in schools, decided to part with him on weaponry. (And the bishops hadn't even begun to advise him on economic policy yet.)

"Haven't they heard about the infallibility of the President?"

May 10, 1983

As we edged closer to armed intervention in Central America, two ghosts flickered into focus: LBJ and the late Slim Pickens as the B-52 pilot in *Dr. Strangelove.*

"There's still time to git off, pardner."

May 17, 1983

"I'm afraid it's dioxin, soaked through from Missouri."

May 20, 1983

U.S. schooling, which hadn't had a healthy kick in the tail since Sputnik went into orbit a quarter-century earlier, suddenly had to face the fact that compared to the educational systems of other "modern" nations, ours is in a sort of Third World of its own.

June 14, 1983

No pantywaist, that Menachem Begin. Surrounded by hostility and disapproval, he was still feeling offensive.

"Custer is my name, and I admire your chutzpah."

June 14, 1983

"Trickle-down" never did work very well in Latin America.

"Mexico is poor again? I was just getting used to being rich."

June 17, 1983

Old-time airline pilots had a motto: "Safety first, comfort second, schedule third." Along came various consumer reports that rated carriers by how closely they kept on time. (I like planes to stay on the ground for foul weather or maintenance.) Then we got de-regulation, dog-eat-dog competition, and the inevitable decay of a proud profession.

"If we try to fix every little thing we'll lose our competitive edge."

July 1, 1983

"Congratulations! You've become a philanthropist."

July 21, 1983

When I drew cartoons protesting the continuing Russian and Japanese slaughter of whales, sometimes I would think, "Well, at least they're probably feeding lots of people on all that blubber." Then Greenpeace traced whalers to a huge mink farm in Siberia which supplies the U.S. and European fur market.

July 26, 1983

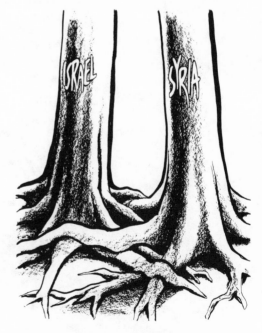

Cedars of Lebanon

July 27, 1983

When Reagan started reconditioning battleships I cheered the idea. Not only are they probably still useful as artillery, but they look impressive steaming into foreign harbors. (Maybe somebody will explain to Reagan's advisers what a harbor really is. It's a wonder the *New Jersey* got out of Nicaraguan waters without losing her keel.)

"Wait'll they learn they're in quicksand."

August 2, 1983

The Face that Launched a Thousand Ships.

August 3, 1983

The Israeli invaders of Lebanon definitely established Arafat as a has-been. It could be argued that he had already become one and they wasted a lot of lives and money for nothing.

"...And here I am wearing my gun while speaking to the U.N...."

"It's no longer almighty, but it's airworthy again."

August 10, 1983

I know that a strong dollar messes up our delicate export balance, but I am a simple-minded traveller who enjoys obsequious headwaiters and hotel clerks.

107

August 23, 1983

"How did you manage that?"

August 24, 1983

They held an election in the Philippines and not many opponents appeared. Those who did got dead quick.

"He's busy oiling the voting machine."

August 25, 1983

When you hear hollow laughter rolling along hospital corridors it comes from patients who can afford rental TV's and have tuned in hospital soaps.

"On TV nobody pays a hospital bill and everybody gets a private room."

August 31, 1983

It has long been illegal to dope horses. We are finally beginning to get around to worrying about human competitors.

"I spell relief, 'S-T-E-R-O-I-D-S.'" 109

September 5, 1983

Starting with the slaughter of the Kulaks and the Moscow purges and continuing through the Katyn forest and the Red Army sitting on the banks of the
Vistula and cheering the Nazi mop-up of Polish patriots, us old folks have
become used to Russian brutality. . . . or so some of us thought until the murder
of 269 Korean airline passengers.

September 14, 1983

The Flight 007 incident showed the world—if further proof was needed—the kind of mind that rules there. The military not only cheerfully admitted premeditation but paraded the airmen who committed the crime.

October 19, 1983

Things such as the Korean airliner affair can cause a certain amount of embarrassment, if only temporary, in some well-meaning circles.

"Ask Moscow not to commit any major atrocities for a few weeks."

111

October 26, 1983

Public outrage over the Flight 007 atrocity probably had an effect upon public acceptance of our Grenada invasion. Anything that looked like an air base with a red star on it begged to be stomped.

"Imperialism!"

October 27, 1983

Gee whiz, and we had only recently been so supportive of British efforts in the Falklands...

"Gee, Maggie Thatcher might at least have wished me a bon voyage."

November 14, 1983

"If we make it red I'll bet Reagan will send a task force."

November 15, 1983

"...Wonder what they do for games."

"He wants to be the only old man in Iran."

November 25, 1983

November 30, 1983

"Trickle-down?"

December 6, 1983

"There's a built-in safety factor. I can only sink so far."

December 20, 1983

Having extricated the *New Jersey* from the mud flats of Central America, we sent her to Lebanon to put some fighting backbone into our neutral peacekeeping stance.

"...Wonder what they'll fire at us if they decide to get involved."

December 22, 1983

Arafat, forgotten but not gone, surfaced again after a short sea voyage out of Lebanon.

"They keep forgetting the oaken stake."

December 28, 1983

Jesse Jackson, running for the Democratic presidential nomination, astounded the nation and confounded his rivals by charming the Syrians into releasing an American pilot they had captured.

January 5, 1984

"Maggie, are you sure 'peacekeeping' is the right word for this?"

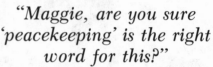

January 26, 1984

At home on the economic front Reagan was back in his own howdah, keen of eye and deadly of aim.

"Did you have to be so brutal?"

118

"To heck with you. I want Jesse Jackson to rescue me."

January 18, 1984

January 11, 1984

*"Maybe we could take out
a second mortgage."*

January 25, 1984

*"I'm ready to make a few concessions
to you ragheads."*

February 15, 1984

President Gemayel of Lebanon, a militant Christian and sometime Israeli client, found his viewpoint broadening as his turf narrowed.

February 21, 1984

Moderation began to seem the order of the day elsewhere in the world, too.

"Under Washington's new guidelines we've bagged our week's limit."

February 22, 1984

Competition tightened up in the Democratic presidential sweepstakes...

"Wrong stuff."

March 15, 1984

...leaving only a couple of heavy-handed featherweights.

Tempering Process

March 16, 1984

Gary Hart, clearly a favorite of modern young Democrats, called Yuppies, and himself, had yet to learn the realities of back-room poker.

March 17, 1984

Nobody had to teach reality to an old apple fancier soon to be appointed Reagan's head cop.

"I'm sure there may be situations in which there may be hungry people..."
(Edwin Meese III)

March 23, 1984

Meese didn't put his benefactors and their families on welfare. Ed was against welfare. He gave them real government jobs.

"Gee, Dad, who did you lend $15,000 to?"

"...For 'tis the sport to have the enginer
Hoist with his own petar..."
(Shakespeare's Hamlet, Act III)

April 12, 1984

Somebody forgot to keep an eye on the CIA again.

April 18, 1984

Smarting from his Nicaraguan embarrassment, the president fell back upon his histrionic talents to divert the nation and send shudders through terrorists worldwide.

Reagan will take offensive against terrorists.
(News Item)

April 20, 1984

Shots were fired at a civilian crowd from the Libyan embassy in London and a British policewoman was killed. Qadhafi brazened out the affair, and the British meekly allowed the killers to leave under diplomatic immunity.

"Argentina didn't have all those oil wells."

April 24, 1984

An old Chiang Kai-shek fan and militant Chinese Nationalist supporter found himself in somewhat halting dialogue with the Mainland. He minced more words than they did.

"Aside from that, how are you?"

May 10, 1984

At last Russia got her chance to pay us back for the 1980 Moscow Olympic boycott. She didn't hurt us as much as we had hurt her, but of course the ones who were really hurt were the athletes of both sides.

"Hey there, Speedy!"

May 11, 1984

"Express Mail" came on with flamboyant ads and all the resources of Uncle Sam, trying to compete in the burgeoning overnight messenger game. But the union-ridden, top-heavy old Postal Service couldn't run on the same track with lean, mean, hungry young hustlers. I tried Express Mail twice. It took almost a week both times.

127

June 12, 1984

"You hate me when I'm strong and despise me when I'm weak."

June 13, 1984

Mondale won the nomination from Gary Hart, and the main event, which already had a predictable outcome, was on.

"Gentlemen, start your pigs."

June 15, 1984

As long as federal authorities, anxious to keep their bureaus as far-reaching as possible, insist upon lumping grass with hard drugs they will have credibility problems. The dumbest teeny-bopper appears to know more about cannabis than the smartest narc.

"But, daddy, you always told me that was the deadly snake."

June 22, 1984

"I think I might be in a little trouble."

"Hey kid—you sure you're old enough to drink?"

July 3, 1984

A number of states began rolling the legal drinking age back upward in the hope that it would reduce DWI casualties.

"...Poor guy vaulted to a new world's record
without a pole."

July 12, 1984

Apparently there were no age restrictions on doping athletes.

July 13, 1984

Geraldine Ferraro became our first woman vice-presidential candidate. Her misfortune was to run with the last New Dealer.

July 17, 1984

As if to cancel his inspired V.P. choice, Mondale selected Bert Lance to run his campaign. Bert had helped Fritz in Georgia. He didn't turn out to be much of an asset now.

Marching through Georgia

July 20, 1984

President Reagan decided to leave it to his opponent to commit himself to increasing everybody's taxes.

"I'll play these."

August 14, 1984

"We're not gonna raise taxes, Ron—we'll just invent some new ones."

133

August 15, 1984

Inevitably, somebody dug up some irregularities in Gerry Ferraro's family finances. Unfailingly, the Democrats counterattacked George Bush, who had been a bit bashful himself about his affairs.

"Show me yours and I'll show you mine."

August 16, 1984

Nobody ever successfully accused Reagan of deftness. His on-mike, off-air radio wisecrack about blowing away Russia was dumb, but it seemed his political critics got more upset about it than the Russians.

"He made a joke about bombing us? How ghastly!"

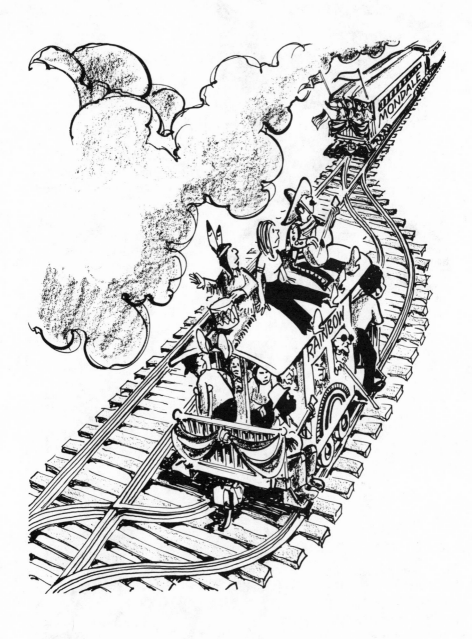

August 17, 1984

Jesse Jackson put together a delightful and colorful coalition which Mondale should have taken on the road. It might even have helped him.

August 28, 1984

Whether it's Jerry Falwell, Menachem Begin, or the Ayatollah Khomeini, these moral majority types share one quality: humorlessness. Without humor you don't know what's ridiculous, including yourself.

Snuffer

August 30, 1984

Once again it was grain contract time with the U.S.S.R., and once again we passed up an opportunity to force the Soviets to hammer a few swords back into plowshares.

"This area is known as the breadbasket of the Soviet Union."

September 6, 1984

Thus far in the presidential campaign Ms. Ferraro was most of the show.

"Saving yourself for the sprint, Fritz?"

September 19, 1984

"Who says religion should stay out of politics and classrooms?"

"Nearer, my God, to Thee."

September 13, 1984

Mondale wasn't the only labor candidate. The teamsters and the air traffic controllers had long ago discovered the joys of Republicanism. However, something had happened to half of this coalition along the way.

September 27, 1984

Reagan's tough anti-soviet stance paid dividends, as he had predicted. The Kremlin, certain now that they would have to deal with this man for another four years, decided to sit down and be comfortable about it. They found Reagan already at the table.

"I used to be allergic, but I took a pill."

September 28, 1984

At last a reasonable man took charge in Israel—at least on a part-time basis.

"You've had enough."

October 2, 1984

"If we're gonna pray in school, why not study in church?"

139

"Thank God I got here in time."

October 9, 1984

It's always funny to hear ardent spenders holler about deficits.

140

October 11, 1984

"Hey, man, how about a little post-fetal concern?"

October 24, 1984

The CIA did it again. This time is was an embarrassing booklet instructing Contras in how to permanently "neutralize" civic officials.

"In future refer to your neutralizers as equalizers or tranquilizers."

October 25, 1984

"I hear China has gone capitalist. Got anything to sell?"

October 30, 1984

A baby called Fae had the misfortune to be born with a bad heart and a nameless baboon had the misfortune to provide her with what appeared, for several weeks, to be a successful replacement. This raised some interesting questions for religious fundamentalists.

142

November 16, 1984

Ravenous barristers have been so successful at drumming up trade that many U.S. manufacturers have given up producing quality merchandise, choosing instead to try to make things lawsuit-proof.

"Sir, I hope you'll let me handle your product liability suit."

November 23, 1984

"War is out. We can't afford more veterans."

November 28, 1984

"*I enjoyed your sermon on soaking the rich. How about property taxes?*"

December 5, 1984

Here came the Catholic bishops again, this time extolling economic egalitarianism . . . while perhaps forgetting the extent and value of their church's tax-exempt real estate holdings.

December 12, 1984

If it isn't the bishops it's those lawyers again. Union Carbide poisoned thousands of people in India, spreading grief over the countryside and great expectations throughout the legal profession.

December 13, 1984

Another busy body was that of Ralph Nader, who decided the sky was unsafe at any altitude. One hopes his hip-shots will not ground air transport as it did the Corvair.

"He's a solution looking for a problem."

Powerplant

December 14, 1984

If Nader ever trained his guns upon the post office I haven't heard of it. What an opportunity to expose a bureaucracy that forces legitimate users to subsidize free loaders!

December 18, 1984

A new face surfaced in the lineup on the Kremlin wall—a comparatively cheery mug belonging to a comparative kid, 54-year-old Mikhail Sergeyevich Gorbachev. When Smiling Mike toured Europe Maggie Thatcher declared him downright cute and the French kissed him copiously.

December 21, 1984

Gorbachev wasn't fooling our defense secretary, who hunkered down and waited for the Soviet public relations blitzkrieg to stop threatening his budget.

Hardened Silo

January 9, 1985

Our president, whose anti-abortion views are well-known, kept the FBI leashed when fanatics started blowing up clinics all over the country. If you get caught carrying TNT across state lines, claim you were on your way to a family planning session.

"Oh, well—pranksters will be pranksters."

January 11, 1985

"Don't worry. The big dough will never let it happen."

January 10, 1985

The New York subway shooting of four muggers brought up anew an old question: if the cops have demonstrated an inability to protect you, do you need a license to protect yourself? If so, they had better loosen up on those licenses.

"Sorry....the law can't protect you or allow you to protect yourself."

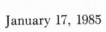
January 17, 1985

"I think we got a safe one here..."

149

"He's all shook up. We must be doing something right."

January 18, 1985

Having bankrupted themselves building enough ICBM's to blow up the galaxy, the Soviets naturally don't relish the prospect of having them made ineffective by a new defense system in space. They regard anything that keeps them from looking down our throats as "offensive."

"My motive is simple. I'm an illegal abortionist."

January 23, 1985

"Attaboy. That's how I got rid of a few million kulaks, too."

January 30, 1985

To the dedicated Marxist food is a weapon. To the dedicated Marxist sex is a weapon. Same with art, music, literature, and sports. Don't those people ever have any fun?

February 1, 1985

The position of the State Department and Immigration Service on Central American refugees is untenable. Try telling it to the judge.

"I sheltered some Salvadoran refugees. What was your crime?"

February 5, 1985

New Zealand's attitude toward nukes is straightforward compared to that of Belgium, which wants us to keep holding the umbrella, but from another location.

"You New Zealanders are so impetuous."

February 7, 1985

Reagan's budget came off the press to a chorus of screams from people who would be pulled off all or some of the federal teat.

"Next."

"Okay...bring on the sacred cows."

February 8, 1985

Nobody can figure out whether David Stockman was retained for his fiscal abilities or his talents as a lightning rod.

Tailgaters

February 20, 1985

The Israelis finally started pulling out of Lebanon. Having been on their backs throughout this book, I'm relieved to surrender my place to somebody else.

155